Bella, with a heart as big as the moon, knew she had to help. She followed the sleigh, which was sprinkling golden stardust, as it slowly descended.

To all the children who find joy and wonder in the magic of Christmas, This book is for you – a celebration of the festive spirit that fills your hearts with warmth and happiness. May these pages add a little more sparkle to your holiday season.

In the spirit of giving, 25% of the proceeds from this book will be donated to support children in need, spreading the joy and love of Christmas far and wide.
Wishing you all a season filled with wonder and delight,

Jolene Ho

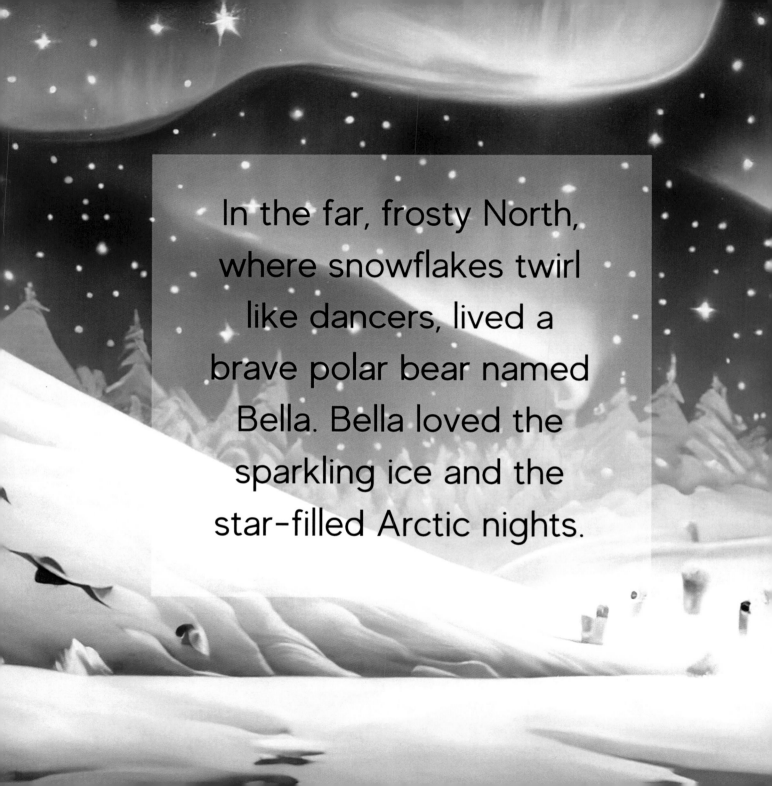

In the far, frosty North, where snowflakes twirl like dancers, lived a brave polar bear named Bella. Bella loved the sparkling ice and the star-filled Arctic nights.

One magical Christmas Eve, as Bella gazed at the stars, she saw a strange sight. Santa's sleigh was soaring through the sky, but it was shaking and not flying right!

The sleigh landed gently, and out stepped Santa, looking quite troubled. "Oh no, my sleigh has broken, and I have so many gifts still to deliver," he sighed.

"Don't worry, Santa! I'll help you," Bella bravely offered. Together, they carefully loaded the gifts onto Bella's strong back, ready to save Christmas.

With a heart full of joy, Bella raced through the snowy night. Santa, with a map in hand, guided her to houses far and near, delivering joy and delight.

At each house, Bella waited patiently outside, listening to the laughter and cheers of children discovering their gifts.

As they traveled, the sky shimmered with the aurora, and Bella felt the warmth of doing good deeds, spreading happiness in the cold Arctic night.

They visited big cities and tiny villages, bringing gifts to every child. Bella's heart swelled with pride, knowing she was part of something magical.

Finally, as the first light of Christmas Day touched the sky, their journey came to an end. Santa thanked Bella, "You're the true hero of Christmas, brave Bella."

Santa gave Bella a special gift
– a silver bell that twinkled like
a star. "This bell is a symbol of
your courage and kindness,"
Santa explained.

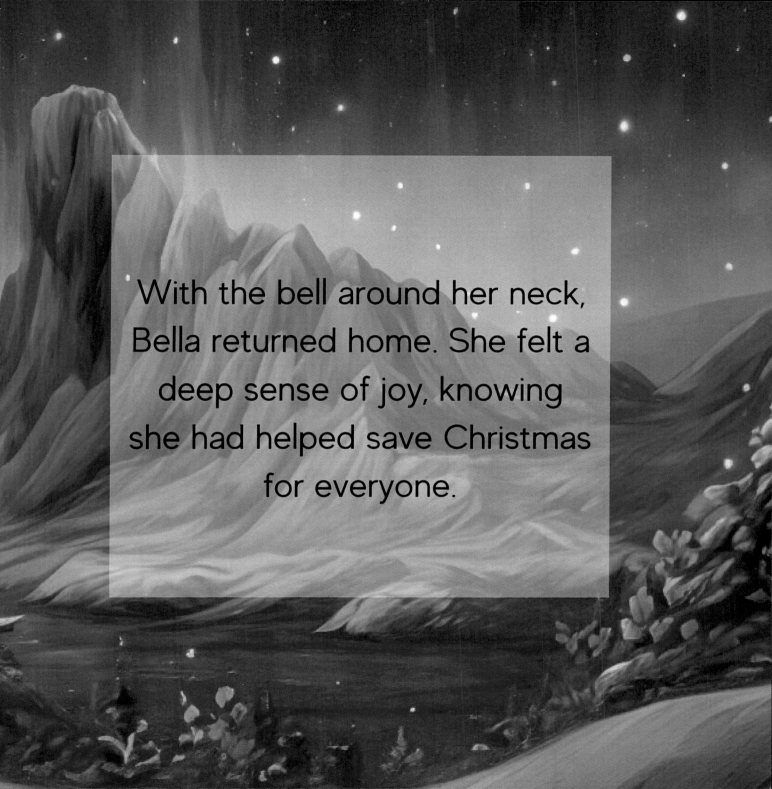

With the bell around her neck, Bella returned home. She felt a deep sense of joy, knowing she had helped save Christmas for everyone.

The other animals in the Arctic gathered around Bella, admiring her shiny bell and listening to her incredible adventure.

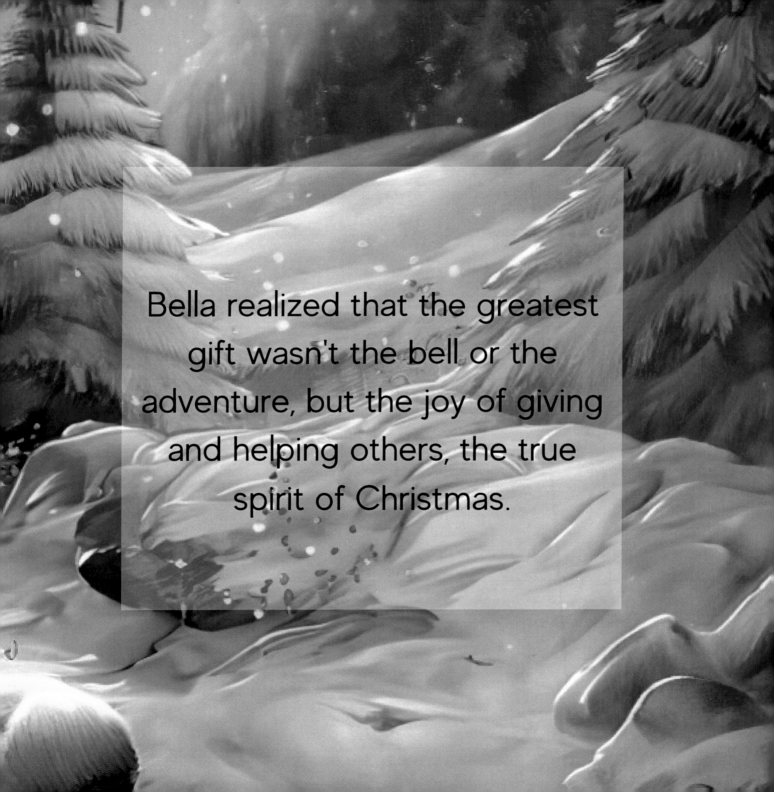

Bella realized that the greatest gift wasn't the bell or the adventure, but the joy of giving and helping others, the true spirit of Christmas.

And every Christmas after, Bella's bell would ring, reminding everyone of the brave polar bear who once saved Christmas.

Made in United States
North Haven, CT
15 December 2023